Your Money at Work

Taxes

ERNESTINE GIESECKE

Heinemann Library
Chicago, Illinois

Designed by Herman Adler Design
Photo Research by John Klein
Printed and bound in the United States by Lake Book Manufacturing, Inc.

07 06
10 9 8 7 6 5 4 3

Library of Congress Cataloging-in-Publication Data
Giesecke, Ernestine, 1945-
   Your money at work–taxes / Ernestine Giesecke.
      p. cm.
Summary: Discusses what taxes are, why we pay taxes, types and classes of taxes, and how the government spends taxes.
Includes bibliographical references (p.   ) and index.
   ISBN 1-58810-494-X (lib. bdg.) – ISBN 1-58810-957-7 (pbk.)
   1. Taxation–United States–Juvenile literature. 2. Taxation–Juvenile literature. [1. Taxation.] I. Title: Your money at work. II. Title.
   HJ2381 .G54 2003
   336.73–dc21

                    2002013752

Acknowledgments
The author and publisher are grateful to the following for permission to reproduce copyright material:
Cover photograph by PhotoDisc/Getty Images.
Title page; p. 4 Stone/Getty Images; p. 5 Corbis; pp. 6, 12, 14, 17, 37, 40, 41 The Granger Collection; p. 7 Courtesy of Jill Birschbach; p. 8 Giraudon/Art Resource; p. 9T Dean Conger/Corbis; p. 9B Dagli Orti/Musee Luxembourgeois Arlon Belgium/Art Archive; p. 11 Scala/Art Resource; pp. 13, 16, 18, 23.T, 28T, 39C, 39R Bettman/Corbis; p. 15 Stephen Jaffe/NewsCom; p. 17 Stephen Tai; p. 20 Swim Ink/Corbis; p. 21 Kevin Lamarque/Reuters Photo Archive/NewsCom; p. 23B Jim West; p. 24 Library of Congress; p. 25 Stockbyte/PictureQuest; p. 28B; p. 29; p. 31 Stapleton Collection/Corbis; p. 32 FEMA; p. 34; p. 35 PictureNet/Corbis; p. 36; p. 39L The Corcoran Gallery of Art/Corbis; p. 42 Felicia Martinez/PhotoEdit; p. 44 The New York Times.

Every effort has been made to contact copyright holders of any material reproduced in this book. Any omissions will be rectified in subsequent printings if notice is given to the publisher.

Note to the Reader: Some words are shown in bold, **like this.** You can find out what they mean by looking in the glossary.

Contents

What Are Taxes? 4

Classes of Taxes 6

Ancient Taxes 8

Taxes in the Middle Ages 10

Taxation and Representation 12

Taxes and the American Colonies 14

Taxes and the New Nation 18

Income Tax Law 20

Social Security and Medicare Taxes 22

Fair Taxes 24

Types of Taxes 26

Collecting Income Taxes 28

Tax Dollars as Revenue 30

Tax Dollars at Work 32

Property Taxes 34

Taxes and Education 36

Paying for Today's Education 42

Follow Your Money .44

Glossary 46

More Books to Read .47

Index 48

Form **W-4**	Employee's Withholding Allowance Certificate	OMB No
Department of the Treasury Internal Revenue Service	▶ For Privacy Act and Paperwork Reduction Act Notice, see page 2.	20

1 Type or print your first name and middle initial Last name		2 Your social security
Home address (number and street or rural route)	3 ☐ Single ☐ Married ☐ Married, but withhold at highe Note: If married, but legally separated, or spouse is a nonresident alien, check	
City or town, state, and ZIP code	4 If your last name differs from that on your social secur check here. You must call 1-800-772-1213 for a new	

5	Total number of allowances you are claiming (from line H above **or** from the applicable worksheet on page 2)	5	
6	Additional amount, if any, you want withheld from each paycheck	6	$
7	I claim exemption from withholding for 2002, and I certify that I meet **both** of the following conditions for exemption:		

- Last year I had a right to a refund of **all** Federal income tax withheld because I had **no** tax liability **and**
- This year I expect a refund of **all** Federal income tax withheld because I expect to have **no** tax liability.

If you meet both conditions, write "Exempt" here . . . . ▶ | 7 |

Under penalties of perjury, I certify that I am entitled to the number of withholding allowances claimed on this certificate, or I am entitled to claim exem
Employee's signature
(Form is not valid

What Are Taxes?

A tax is a payment, required by law, designed to pay for government. Individuals, groups of people, and businesses pay taxes. In the past, grain, wine, farm produce, and **services** were accepted as payment for taxes. Today, most taxes are paid in the form of money. Some taxes are for a specific amount. This means that everyone who pays the tax pays the same amount. Other taxes are tied to a tax rate or **percentage.**

Know It

Taxes transfer **resources,** such as money, from individuals to a government. A government uses those resources to provide goods and services to the taxpayers.

People pay taxes so that their government can supply **goods** or services they may not be able to purchase on their own. For example, local governments use tax money to pay for teachers' **salaries,** police and fire protection, water and sewer services, and garbage collection. National governments use money from taxes to pay for education, health programs, highways, and national defense.

There are rules about how taxes work. First, the law requires taxes. Second, the taxpayer does not receive a specific item, such as public land,

Local governments use tax money to buy cloth for uniforms and equipment for fire fighting. Taxes also pay the firefighters' salaries.

Taxing vocabulary

Many words can be used to describe money collected from individuals used to support a government. *Duty*, **levy, toll,** *dues, tribute,* and *fee* are some of the synonyms for taxes. Because the word *tax* often makes people uneasy, some taxes were identified by names specifically chosen to disguise the fact that they were, indeed, taxes. For example, some English kings demanded a *benevolence* from their subjects. The benevolence was a mandatory gift of money. Another example, *ship money*, was actually a tax collected from coastal cities and counties so that the English government would defend them in times of war.

in exchange for the tax he or she pays. Third, taxes are collected for the benefit of all taxpayers. That is, an individual taxpayer is required to pay even if he or she does not receive any direct benefit from the tax dollar. For example, in the United States every taxpayer helps pay for hurricane relief, even if the taxpayer does not live in an area where hurricanes occur.

All governments collect taxes. In some cases, taxes increase so that the government can provide additional services. Throughout history, governments at war raised taxes in order to pay for the food, clothing, and weapons the army needed. In other cases, greedy or cruel rulers raised taxes in order to increase their own personal wealth.

The main offices of the United States tax collector are located in Washington, D.C., the nation's capital.

In ancient China, citizens paid their taxes with large sheets of pressed tea. Indigenous people living on islands near Australia paid taxes with sharks' teeth.

Classes of Taxes

There are two classes of taxes, direct and indirect. A direct tax can be described as a tax upon an individual. Generally, direct taxes are based on a person's ability to pay the tax. The amount of a person's **income,** or how much a person owes, are measures of his or her ability to pay.

Income tax is an example of a direct tax. Another example of a direct tax is a spending tax, a tax on all income that is not saved. Other direct taxes include **inheritance** taxes—a tax on the amount received by an **heir**—and estate taxes—a tax on the total amount of money left by a person who died. Another direct tax is the gift tax. This tax, paid by the person who gives the gift, applies to property that is given away during the person's lifetime. Property tax is also a direct tax.

An indirect tax applies to a **service** or **privilege,** rather than a person. An indirect tax is a tax that can be shifted depending on who is using a service.

In 1766, William Pitt, Prime Minister of England, stated his government's position on indirect taxes. It was likely the position of most governments:

There is a method by which you can tax the last rag from the back, and the last bite from the mouth, without causing a murmur against high taxes, and that is, to tax a great many articles of daily use and necessity so indirectly that the people will pay them and not know it. Their grumbling will then be of hard times, but they will not know that the hard times are caused by taxation.

Legal transactions such as the sale of houses are subject to taxes. To prove the tax has been paid, the document is stamped.

TRUSTEE'S DEED

THIS INDENTURE, dated **April 30, 2002** between **LASALLE BANK NATIONAL ASSOCIATION,** a National Banking Association, successor trustee to American National Bank and Trust Company of Chicago duly authorized to accept and execute trusts within the State of Illinois, not personally but as Trustee under the provisions of a deed or deeds in trust duly recorded and delivered to said Bank in pursuance of a certain Trust Agreement . dated **May 13, 1999** and known as Trust Number ▓▓▓▓▓ party of the first part, and ▓▓▓▓▓▓▓▓▓▓▓▓▓▓▓▓▓ party/parties of the second part.

(Reserved for Recorders Use Only)

WITNESSETH, that said party of the first part, in consideration of the sum of TEN ($10.00) Dollars and other good and valuable consideration in hand paid, does hereby convey and **QUIT-CLAIM** unto said party/parties of the second part, the following described real estate, situated in **Cook** County, Illinois, to-wit:

SEE EXHIBIT A ATTACHED HERETO FOR LEGAL DESCRIPTION AND SUBJECT TO PROVISIONS

Commonly Known As: _____ Evanston, Illinois 60202

Property Index Numbers: ___30-211___

together with the tenements and appurtenances thereunto belonging.

TO HAVE AND TO HOLD, the same unto said party of the second part, and to the proper use, benefit and behoof, forever, of said party of the second part.

This deed is executed by the party of the first part, as Trustee, as aforesaid, pursuant to and in the exercise of the power and authority granted to and vested in it by the terms of said Deed or Deeds in Trust and the provisions of said Trust Agreement above mentioned, and of every other power and authority thereunto enabling. This deed is made subject to the liens of all trust deeds and/or mortgages upon said real estate, if any, recorded or registered in said county.

IN WITNESS WHEREOF, said party of the first part has caused its corporate seal to be hereto affixed, and has caused its name to be signed to these presents by one of its officers, the day and year first above written.

LASALLE BANK NATIONAL ASSOCIATION, as trustee and not personally,

By: _Harriet Denisewicz_

Harriet Denisewicz, Trust Officer

Prepared By:
Harriet Denisewicz (tmf)
JLASALLE BANK NATIONAL ASSOCIATION,
135 S. LASALLE ST
CHICAGO IL 60603

CITY OF EVANSTON 011078
Real Estate Transfer Tax
City Clerk's Office
PAID MAY 1 3 2002 AMOUNT $ _750.00_

Agent _MP_

Rev. 8/00

document stamp

The general sales tax and selective sales tax are examples of indirect tax. The government collects the tax from store owners based on the dollar amount of the **goods** sold. The store owner, however, collects the tax from each customer who makes a purchase. The store owner adds an amount equal to the tax he or she must pay to the price of the goods. The government then collects the tax from the store owner.

A general sales tax is applied to nearly all consumer purchases. In some cases, all items are taxed at the same rate. In other cases, different items are taxed at different rates. The rate of indirect taxes may be stated as a **percent** of the price of the item, such as three percent, or as a unit tax, such as one cent per gallon. Often, general sales tax is not applied to necessary items such as food or prescription medicine.

Selective sales tax includes **excise** taxes— taxes placed on specific products such as wine, liquor, salt, coffee, or tea. Other indirect taxes include taxes on automobiles and legal transactions.

Oliver Wendell Holmes, a past United States Supreme Court justice once said, "Taxes are what we pay for a civilized society."

Ancient Taxes

Before money was common people **bartered,** or exchanged items with each other. In barter **economies,** governments collected taxes in the form of the products or the **goods** produced by a taxpayer.

Some of the earliest recorded taxes were collected in ancient Egypt. Tax collectors were scribes. They kept written records of who owned farms, as well as the size of each farm. Scribes used this information to figure out how much tax a farmer owed. The amount of land the farmer had, as well as the products of the land, such as corn, wheat, and livestock were taxed.

Know It

A land, or property, tax is one of the easiest taxes to carry out because ownership is difficult to hide.

Bartering was also taxed. **Merchants** and craftspeople paid taxes on most of the things they traded, such as oil, bronze, and bricks. Merchants also paid a tax that was called a license fee, so they could sell **linen.** Fishers paid for the right to catch fish in certain waterways.

In addition, Egyptians had their **income** taxed. The pharaohs used the money from taxes to build public buildings and pyramids, as well as feed and clothe armies.

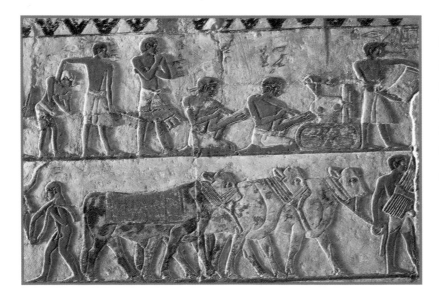

Scribes carefully counted and recorded the number of livestock a person had. That number would determine the amount of tax owed to the government.

The Great Wall of China, now more than 2,000 years old, was once long enough to reach from London to Chicago (just under 4,000 miles; 6,437 kilometers). The wall was built with the world's earliest form of taxes—human labor.

In ancient Rome there was a tax on the amount of money a person spent. The tax applied to all income that was not placed in savings. Another tax applied to goods brought into the **Roman Empire** to sell. All Romans paid a head tax. The head tax was the same amount for all citizens, whether they were rich or poor. Rome introduced a one-**percent** sales tax during the reign of Julius Caesar.

The Roman Empire relied primarily on head and land taxes. Money from these taxes paid for the huge army, as well as for public works such as sports arenas, temples, amphitheaters, and roads built throughout the empire.

Tax collectors worked throughout the Roman Empire, making sure that people paid what they owed.

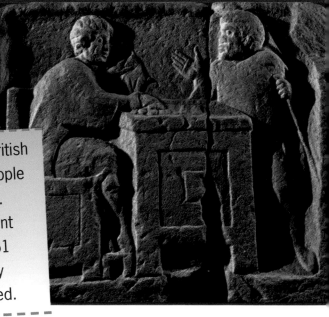

One of the earliest tax revolts occurred in the British Isles when it was part of the Roman Empire. People in Britain did not want to pay tax to the Romans. An army of more than 100,000 soldiers was sent to kill every Roman soldier within 100 miles (161 kilometers). But Rome sent more soldiers. They captured London and 80,000 British people died.

Taxes in the Middle Ages

The **Roman Empire's** wars and crushing taxes, plus its forceful way of collecting taxes, played a part in its downfall. After the Roman Empire fell, a system of smaller-scale kingdoms took its place. However, these smaller governments still demanded taxes.

Most kings controlled only the land they owned. A king might give a piece of land to a **lord.** In return, the lord promised to be loyal to the king. Within his own territory—which often included a manor—a lord had several duties. He had to supply **knights** to the king. He also had to collect taxes and fines from peasants, farmers, and villagers who lived on his land.

This pyramid represents the system of government called feudalism. During the Middle Ages, kings would give land to lords who would in turn provide knights to defend the king's territory. Peasants provided the **goods** and **services** for everyone above them.

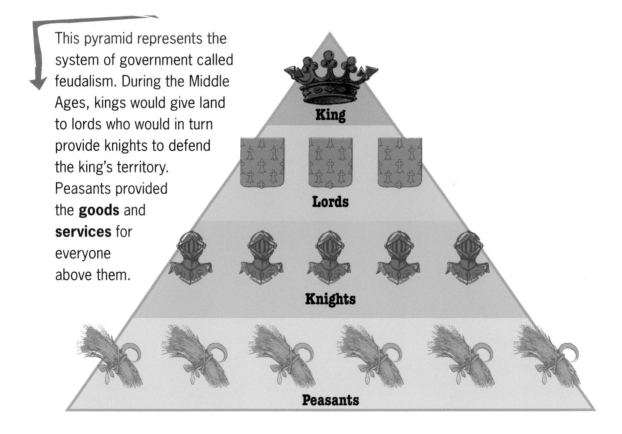

King

Lords

Knights

Peasants

The direct head tax from the Roman Empire was no longer in effect. But there were many other types of taxes. In some cases, it was possible to pay a tax as a substitute for serving in the lord's army.

There were many fees for selling things in a market. There were **tolls** for using bridges and roads. There was a death tax for some people, and peasants paid a relief tax for events like marriage. Lords and kings taxed people living in villages and cities. People paid taxes on certain foods and drinks. Taxes on land and houses soon spread.

In China during the Shang Dynasty (1523–1027 B.C.E.), there was a tax system called the well field. Nine farming fields were cut from a square of land. Each field measured about 100 acres. A family worked each of the outside fields. All the farmers worked the ninth field. They would give the crops from the ninth field to the government as payment for taxes due.

1	2	3
4	9	5
6	7	8

Manor life

In a kingdom, the land a lord controlled was called a manor. In general, a manor consisted of a manor house, one or more villages, and as much as several thousand acres of land. The land may have included farms, forests, and fields. The fields were divided into strips.

About one-third of the land was for the lord. Peasants were expected to work in the lord's fields. Peasants were also expected to clear forests, cut firewood, and build roads and bridges. Peasants could work their own fields in any free time they might have. The manor system was common throughout much of Europe. There was a similar system in Japan. There, shoguns and samurai were the Japanese names for lords and knights.

Taxation and Representation

During the Middle Ages, the **boundaries** between lands held by **lords** and kings were often fought over. Some kings increased their lands, swallowing up smaller manors. In Britain, a central government began to gather power.

By 1200, the British king faced large **debts.** Taxes were needed to pay for wars. As the king demanded more taxes from his lords, the lords became worried about their rights. They banded together to get a promise of **liberties** from the king. These liberties are listed in a famous document called the Magna Carta. Magna Carta means "great charter" in Latin. Among the liberties it lists is the right not to be taxed without consent:

> *No scutage* [tax] *or aid shall be imposed in our kingdom unless by common counsel of our kingdom, …*

The Magna Carta, created in 1215, listed other liberties in addition to those referring to taxes. Among the most important was that the church should be "free" from interference from the King.

The Magna Carta is one of the first official documents to say that taxes should not be **levied** without the consent of those being taxed. People who are taxed should have a say in what happens in a country. In other words, there should be no taxation without **representation**. This basic liberty concerning taxes played a central role in the history of the British **colonies** in North America.

Tax protesters

In the 1000s, Lady Godiva, wife of an English Earl, became famous as a tax protester. Lady Godiva pleaded with her husband to lower taxes. According to legend, he said he would do so on the day she would ride naked through the local town. She did, covered only by her long hair. Her husband kept his word and lowered taxes.

In the 1300s, the country of Austria refused to recognize Switzerland's independence. Many Swiss people, including a man named William Tell, refused to pay a tax demanded by Austria. For his punishment, Tell was ordered to shoot an apple from his son's head using a crossbow. He succeeded, but was later arrested on separate charges. His actions supposedly helped encourage people to revolt against Austria.

Taxes and the American Colonies

During the 1600s and early 1700s, **merchants** in the British **colonies** in North America started successfully trading with Dutch and French merchants. This led the British government to try to control trade by making laws and by ordering taxes on things brought into the colonies.

Colonists largely ignored the laws. They continued to ship **goods** as they pleased. For a while, they also ignored the taxes. They would pay off officials if they needed. The British placed taxes on items bought from countries that were not controlled by Britain. While the taxes did produce **revenue,** its main purpose was to control trade by making it more desirable and affordable to trade with Britain. For example, because of the tax, molasses from the French West Indies cost more than molasses from the British West Indies. Many colonists felt that it was okay for the British to control trade.

However, in the 1760s, Britain wanted to find a way to pay for the French and Indian War in North America.

This stamp is one of the many stamps manufactured for the Stamp Act. Colonists felt that the Stamp Act was "taxation without **representation,**" and so it violated their **civil rights.**

In 1765, **Parliament** passed the Stamp Act. The Stamp Act was a direct tax. It required that printed materials—including newspapers, playing cards, legal documents, and land titles—carry a stamp. Colonists had to purchase stamps from officials. Because this tax was clearly designed to raise revenue, colonists felt it was **unconstitutional**.

Angry colonists held a meeting in December 1765. At the meeting, known as the Stamp Act Congress, colonists indicated that taxes could not be collected without their consent or the consent of their representatives. But the colonists had no representatives in Parliament. Their home was in the colonies—far from Great Britain—it would be impossible for them to be represented in Parliament.

The Stamp Act Congress said:

> …*That it is inseparably essential to the freedom of a people, … that no taxes should be imposed on them, but with their own consent, given personally, or by their representatives.*

> …*That the people of these colonies are not, and from their local circumstances cannot be, represented in the House of Commons in Great Britain.*

The Stamp Act Congress requested that the Stamp Act be **repealed.**

British taxes levied on the colonies

Navigation Act, 1660
Goods such as sugar, indigo, and tobacco could be shipped only to other British colonies. Taxes applied to the export of these products.

Revenue Act, 1673
"Plantation duty" imposed on certain American exports.

Molasses Act, 1733
High **tariff** placed on molasses imported into the colonies from non-British-controlled countries. Sugar and rum were also taxed.

Sugar Act, 1764
Revision of the Molasses Act. Duty on molasses was cut in half, import duties were placed on foreign sugar, wine, and other products. High sales tax was placed on salt, beer, and liquor.

Stamp Act, 1765
Direct tax placed on all newspapers printed in the colonies and most legal documents.

Stamp Act repealed, 1766

Townshend Act, 1767
Duties imposed on glass, paint, lead, paper, and tea imported into the colonies.

Townshend Act repealed, 1770
A small duty on tea remained.

Tea Act, 1773
East India Company was given a tax break in order to sell tea in the colonies cheaper than its competitors.

Salt tax

The British tax on tea was not the only tax that drove people to rebel. Taxes on salt have been responsible, in part, for rebellions and revolutions in ancient China, eighteenth-century France, and colonial India. Why salt? Everyone needs salt to live and everyone uses it at about the same rate. That's part of the problem—rich and poor were taxed the same amount. But the salt tax takes a greater fraction of a poor person's **income** than it does a rich person's income.

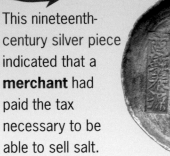

This nineteenth-century silver piece indicated that a **merchant** had paid the tax necessary to be able to sell salt.

Seventy-five years ago, Mahatma Gandhi led a 200-mile (322-kilometer) march to the Arabian Sea to collect untaxed salt for India's poor. The march was a protest against British rule of India.

As a result of the Stamp Act, **colonists** harassed British stamp officials and tax collectors. Colonists even used violence to stop the selling of stamps. In addition, colonists organized a boycott. This meant they refused to buy British **goods.**

Parliament repealed the Stamp Act in 1766. However, Parliament used the opportunity to declare that its authority to tax the colonies was the same as its authority to tax all lands that were part of Great Britain.

Know It

Colonists rebelled against being taxed without **representation.**

In 1767, British Prime Minister Townshend developed the Townshend Act. Townshend thought he had a plan for collecting taxes from the colonists without upsetting them. The new tax was on imports into the colonies, such as tea, paint, glass, paper, and lead (needed to make windows). But the colonists soon realized that the Townshend Act—just like the Stamp Act before it—was designed to raise **revenue.**

Colonial leaders wanted the Townshend Act repealed. They organized another boycott. Great numbers of colonists refused to import or use the taxed goods. The British repealed the Townshend Act in 1770, except for a small tax on tea.

Three years later, Parliament passed the Tea Act. The Tea Act allowed the East India Company, a British company, to sell its tea at a lower price than its competitors—even with the tea tax. At the same time, Parliament hoped to **levy** direct revenue taxes on the colonies. Colonists became angry. The Tea Act seemed like yet another way to tax the colonies.

On December 16, 1773, a group of colonists staged a tax protest. Disguised as Mohawk Indians, they boarded three cargo ships bearing 342 chests of East India tea. The protesters dumped the entire shipment of tea into Boston Harbor. This tax protest signaled the beginning of the American Revolution.

During the Boston Tea Party about 50 colonists, led by Samuel Adams and including Paul Revere, threw 342 chests of tea into the harbor.

Taxes and the New Nation

After the Revolutionary War, the leaders of the new United States carefully listed the responsibilities of the new government. At first, taxing was not one of them. For its **income,** the new government relied on borrowing money, selling public lands, and voluntary donations from the states.

The Constitution of the United States, passed in 1788, gave the **federal** government the power to collect certain taxes. Among the first taxes were **tariffs,** or taxes on imported **goods.** In addition, Congress **levied excise** taxes on items such as alcohol, tobacco, carriages, property sold at auction, refined sugar, and slaves. The **revenue** from these taxes went to repay **debts** from the Revolutionary War.

Know It

For many years, the United States government relied on tariffs as its only source of income.

Whiskey Rebellion

The leaders of the new nation carefully chose which items would be taxed. Even so, the country had to deal with a tax rebellion. In 1794, farmers in western Pennsylvania, Maryland, and Virginia opposed a tax on whiskey. Their most valuable crops were corn and rye, two ingredients used to make whiskey. The whiskey tax would reduce the amount of grain they could sell.

Other people believed the taxes were a necessary source of money for the government, no matter what was being taxed. President George Washington used an army of nearly 13,000 soldiers to put down the rebellion.

When they wanted to pay for the cost of the War of 1812, the federal government passed its first sales tax. Taxed items included refined sugar, gold, silverware, jewelry, and watches.

In 1817, Congress **repealed** all existing excise and sales taxes. The government relied on tariffs for its revenue. By 1832, tariffs accounted for nine-tenths of the government's revenue.

In the 1860s, Congress searched for a way to pay for the Civil War. Meanwhile, ordinary citizens began to resent tariffs. People began to push for a tax on the wealthy, such as an income tax. When Congress enacted the Tax Act of 1862, the country had its first tax on income. The tax specified two different rates. Income above $600 was taxed at a rate of three **percent;** income above $10,000 was taxed at a rate of five percent. The Commissioner of Revenue stated:

> *The people of this country have accepted it with cheerfulness, to meet a temporary exigency* [situation], *and it has excited no serious complaint in its administration.*

When even more money was needed to pay for the war, Congress passed the Tax Act of 1864. The tax rates increased: 5 percent for income between $600 and $5,000; 7.5 percent for income between $5,001 and $10,000; and 10 percent on income above $10,000. The increase in rates for higher income was an attempt to make the income tax rate related to a person's ability to pay.

Dog tax

While the federal government relied on only one kind of tax, local governments relied on a variety of taxes. For example, during the late 1800s, some governments required dog owners to pay a tax for each dog they owned. Working dogs or farm dogs were sometimes not taxed. To prove that the tax had been paid, the owner was given a tag for the dog to wear.

Income Tax Law

Once the Civil War was over, taxpayers did not want to continue paying **income** taxes. Even though Congress reduced the rates, people still called for an end to the tax. So, in 1872, the income tax was **repealed.** After the repeal, the government again depended on **tariffs** as its major source of income.

After about 30 years, the tariffs and **excise** taxes no longer provided enough income to support the activities of a growing and more powerful government. In addition, poorer taxpayers pointed out that they paid a greater part of their income in taxes than rich people. People pressured Congress to create a more fair tax. They wanted a tax that would take into account the taxpayer's ability to pay. In response, Congress proposed an **amendment** to the Constitution. It gave the government the power to put an income tax in place. Congress designed the income tax so that people with a greater income would pay a greater tax rate.

Know It

The Internal Revenue Service is the nation's tax collection agency. It carries out the Internal Revenue Code put into place by Congress.

In 1913, two-thirds of the states had approved the Sixteenth Amendment to the Constitution, and it became law. The **federal** government could now impose an income tax law based on the ability to pay. At the time of the amendment, taxpayers with incomes from $4,000 to $20,000, paid a rate of one **percent.** The highest rate, imposed in 1913 to fund World War I, was seven percent. But, only four years later, the top income tax bracket jumped to 67 percent!

In 1939, as World War II began, about fifteen percent of Americans paid income tax. Most Americans paid their taxes every three months. This meant

During World War II, the government tried many different ways to encourage average Americans to save their money so that they would have enough money to make their tax payments. They even turned to popular cartoon characters, like Donald Duck, for help.

Taxing changes

Over the years, the amount of tax owed by an individual has varied greatly. Each year the government sends instructions detailing any changes along with the blank tax forms.

Federal Income Tax Comparisons

Income	Single person				
	2000	1999	1998	1995	1975
$10,000	$391	$428	$ 457	$540	$1,506
$20,000	$1,916	$1,939	$1,858	$2,040	$4,153
$30,000	$3,416	$3,439	$3,458	$3,573	$8,018
$40,000	$5,765	$4,939	$5,595	$6,373	$12,765
$50,000	$8,593	$7,528	$6,549	$9,173	$18,360

taxpayers were very aware of the amount going to the government. In 1943, the government introduced payroll taxes. By taking tax out of every paycheck, the government hoped to make paying taxes less unpleasant. In addition, payroll taxes increased the number of people paying taxes. By 1945, at the end of the war, 80 percent of U.S. families paid income tax.

In the 50 years since payroll taxes were introduced, the federal government has sometimes increased and sometimes decreased tax rates. Sometimes it has changed the tax system. Other times, it has tried to **reform** the system.

The Economic Growth and Tax Relief Reconciliation Act of 2001, being signed in the photo above, included many tax cuts. It offered benefits to taxpayers and tax cuts so that some families no longer had to pay any income tax.

Social Security and Medicare Taxes

In addition to paying **income** tax, most workers also pay **Social Security** tax and **Medicare** tax. These taxes are designed to provide **insurance** for certain groups of people.

The Social Security tax, also known as the Federal Insurance Contributions Act (FICA) tax, is an insurance program. It is designed to pay **retired** workers income. Workers and **employers** pay equal amounts of the FICA tax. Medicare tax pays for hospital insurance.

FICA and Medicare taxes are aimed at easing the hardships that come with death, disability, and old age. Before the 1900s, most people in the United States lived and worked on farms and usually lived with an **extended family.** This meant that the old and disabled were looked after. The situation changed when cities grew and more people lived in cities than on farms.

In the 1930s, many people were not able to find work. These people also needed help to live. That help came from the government.

Know It

FICA tax pays for old age and disability insurance. Medicare tax pays for hospital insurance.

Taxes for charity

Collecting taxes to provide for the poor has been done for hundreds of years. Part of Christian tithe or Islamic zakat was to help the poor. Towns in Germany passed poor laws in 1520. In the 1500s in England, churches were required to collect local taxes to give relief to those who could not work. At the end of the 1700s, the **Prussian** states used taxes to provide food and shelter for those who could not support themselves.

President Franklin D. Roosevelt signed the Social Security Act in 1935.

The Social Security Act authorizes the government to provide cash payments to citizens for a variety of conditions:

We can never insure one-hundred percent of the population against one-hundred percent of the hazards and vicissitudes [changes] of life. But we have tried to frame a law which will give some measure of protection to the average citizen and to his family against the loss of a job and against poverty-ridden old age.

About 140 countries have some type of social security tax. Nearly all these countries provide benefits for work-related injury, and old age and survivors' pensions. More than half of the countries also help people who are ill.

The Social Security Act has been changed several times since it originally passed in 1935. Today it covers more workers and, provides a wider range of benefits. The amount of tax paid in and the amount of benefits paid out have also changed over the years.

The amount of benefits this senior citizen receives depends on how long he worked, how much money he earned, and his age.

Fair Taxes

Many taxpayers realize that governments collect taxes in order to provide **services** that taxpayers could not provide for themselves. So, while they may not like paying taxes, taxpayers understand the need for taxes. However, nearly all taxpayers would feel better about paying taxes if they could be sure the taxes were fair. Experts who study taxes have developed a list of four characteristics of fair tax. Taxes with these characteristics are more likely to be fair than taxes without them.

First, a tax should be inexpensive and easy to collect. The cost of collecting a tax should be as low as possible. Tax laws and **regulations** should be written so that all taxpayers can understand them. The meaning of a tax law should be clear to both the taxpayer and the tax collector. Confusing tax laws often result in error or dishonesty.

Second, a tax should be direct. It should be collected from the person who pays the tax. Along with this characteristic is the idea that the person paying the tax should receive some benefit from the tax. For example,

Know It

A fair tax is inexpensive to collect, direct, shows no favorites, and does not harm the **economy.**

Thousands of cartoons have poked fun at taxes. This cartoon first appeared in 1929.

TRY TO MAKE OUT MY THEORY AND YOUR INCOME TAX WORK WILL LOOK SIMPLE!

drivers paying **toll** road fees receive a benefit from the collected tax because governments use the tolls to build and fix the roads.

Third, a tax law should have no special exceptions, or tax loopholes. Every time one taxpayer uses an exception or loophole, all other taxpayers must make up the loss of tax dollars. In addition, a tax should correspond to the taxpayer's ability to pay. For example, those with a greater **income** should pay a greater portion, or **percentage**, of income taxes.

Finally, a tax should not have an undesirable outcome. Taxes might result in people making choices that are different because of the tax. Suppose a government placed a big tax on books. People would avoid buying books to avoid having to pay the tax.

Most governments try to find a way to collect taxes with as little complaint as possible from taxpayers. During the 1600s, the financial advisor to King Louis XIV of France, Jean Baptiste Colbert, compared taxpayers to geese. He offered the following observation of tax collection:

"The art of taxation consists in so plucking the goose as to obtain the largest possible amount of feathers with the smallest possible amount of hissing."

Types of Taxes

There are two types of taxes that are related to a person's **income**: regressive and progressive. Regressive tax is the same amount for people of all incomes. Progressive taxes change, depending on how much income a person makes.

Tariffs and **excise** taxes take a larger part of a person's income the less money they make. These taxes are regressive. Sales and property taxes are also regressive. For instance, a seven **percent** sales tax on a car might represent a large part of a working person's income. But to a rich person, the same amount of money would be less noticeable. Tobacco, gasoline, and liquor sales taxes are also considered regressive. Because it

Know It

In ancient Sparta, everyone had to fast for one day and then pay a tax of 100 percent of the food that they would have eaten!

Regressive tax

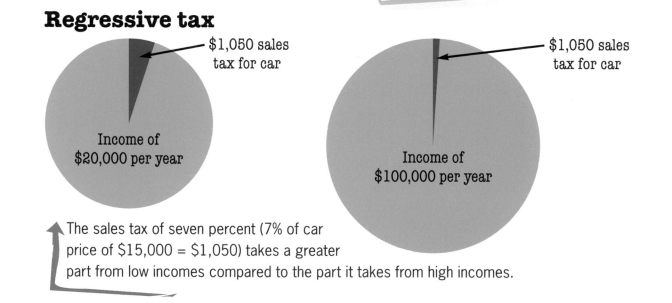

$1,050 sales tax for car

Income of $20,000 per year

$1,050 sales tax for car

Income of $100,000 per year

The sales tax of seven percent (7% of car price of $15,000 = $1,050) takes a greater part from low incomes compared to the part it takes from high incomes.

is the same for everyone, sales tax in each state places a greater burden on low income families. This is why some states do not charge sales tax on medicine or food.

Progressive tax

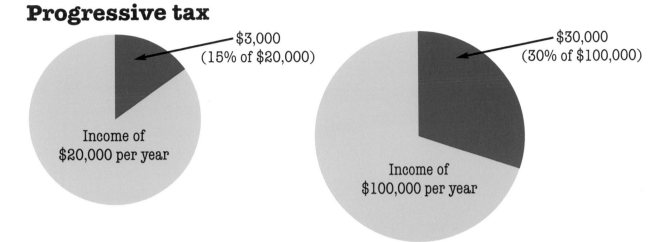

$3,000
(15% of $20,000)

Income of
$20,000 per year

$30,000
(30% of $100,000)

Income of
$100,000 per year

A graduated income tax rate changes depending on the amount of a person's income. Lower incomes are taxed at a low rate, while higher incomes are taxed at a greater rate. Income tax is a progressive tax because it takes a greater part of income from high-income groups than from low-income groups.

If taxes were proportional, all taxpayers would pay the same percentage of their income in taxes no matter what their income. If the tax rate of a proportional tax was ten percent, all taxpayers would pay ten percent of their income.

Proportional tax

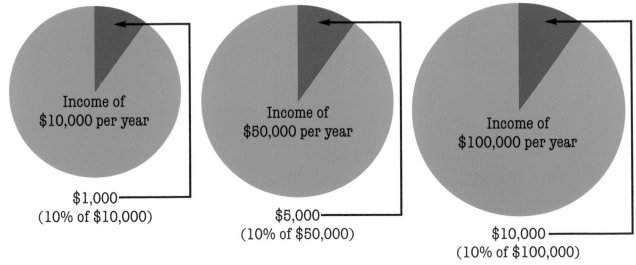

Income of
$10,000 per year

$1,000
(10% of $10,000)

Income of
$50,000 per year

$5,000
(10% of $50,000)

Income of
$100,000 per year

$10,000
(10% of $100,000)

Collecting Income Taxes

Every year in the United States, the date of April 15 is when **federal** and state **income** taxes are due. But the tax due date is the last in a series of steps the Internal **Revenue** Service (IRS) takes to collect personal income tax.

United States citizens who receive an income are required to have a social security number. The Internal Revenue Service uses this number as a taxpayer identification number.

The IRS requires that your **employer withhold,** or hold back, part of your pay. On your first day at work, your employer will ask you to complete an "Employee's Withholding Allowance Certificate," also known as a W-4 form. Completing the form gives your employer permission to withhold part of your pay. The information on the form tells your employer how much of your pay he or she should withhold.

Form W-4 (2002)

Purpose. Complete Form W-4 so your employer can withhold the correct Federal income tax from your pay. Because your tax situation may change, you may want to refigure your withholding each year.

Exemption from withholding. If you are exempt, complete only lines 1, 2, 3, 4, and 7 and sign the form to validate it. Your exemption for 2002 expires February 16, 2003. See Pub. 505, Tax Withholding and Estimated Tax.

Note: You cannot claim exemption from withholding if **(a)** your income exceeds $750 and includes more than $250 of unearned income (e.g., interest and dividends) and **(b)** another person can claim you as a dependent on their tax return.

Basic instructions. If you are not exempt, complete the **Personal Allowances Worksheet** below. The worksheets on page 2 adjust your withholding allowances based on itemized deductions, certain credits, adjustments to

income, or two-earner/two-job situations. Complete all worksheets that apply. **However, you may claim fewer (or zero) allowances.**

Head of household. Generally, you may claim head of household filing status on your tax return only if you are unmarried and pay more than 50% of the costs of keeping up a home for yourself and your dependent(s) or other qualifying individuals. See line E below.

Tax credits. You can take projected tax credits into account in figuring your allowable number of withholding allowances. Credits for child or dependent care expenses and the child tax credit may be claimed using the **Personal Allowances Worksheet** below. See Pub. 919, How Do I Adjust My Tax Withholding? for information on converting your other credits into withholding allowances.

Nonwage income. If you have a large amount of nonwage income, such as interest or dividends, consider making estimated tax payments using Form 1040-ES, Estimated Tax for Individuals. Otherwise, you may owe additional tax.

Two earners/two jobs. If you have a working spouse or more than one job, figure the total number of allowances you are entitled to claim on all jobs using worksheets from only one Form W-4. Your withholding usually will be most accurate when all allowances are claimed on the Form W-4 for the highest paying job and zero allowances are claimed on the others.

Nonresident alien. If you are a nonresident alien, see the **Instructions for Form 8233** before completing this Form W-4.

Check your withholding. After your Form W-4 takes effect, use Pub. 919 to see how the dollar amount you are having withheld compares to your projected total tax for 2002. See Pub. 919, especially if you used the **Two-Earner/Two-Job Worksheet** on page 2 and your earnings exceed $125,000 (Single) or $175,000 (Married).

Recent name change? If your name on line 1 differs from that shown on your social security card, call 1-800-772-1213 for a new social security card.

Personal Allowances Worksheet (Keep for your records.)

A Enter "1" for **yourself** if no one else can claim you as a dependent . . . . **A** ___

B Enter "1" if:
- You are single and have only one job; or
- You are married, have only one job, and your spouse does not work; or
- Your wages from a second job or your spouse's wages (or the total of both) are $1,000 or less. } . . **B** ___

C Enter "1" for your **spouse.** But, you may choose to enter "-0-" if you are married and have either a working spouse or more than one job. (Entering "-0-" may help you avoid having too little tax withheld.) . . . . **C** ___

D Enter number of **dependents** (other than your spouse or yourself) you will claim on your tax return . . . . **D** ___

E Enter "1" if you will file as **head of household** on your tax return (see conditions under **Head of household** above) . . **E** ___

F Enter "1" if you have at least $1,500 of **child or dependent care expenses** for which you plan to claim a credit . . **F** ___
(**Note:** Do **not** include child support payments. See Pub. 503, Child and Dependent Care Expenses, for details.)

G **Child Tax Credit** (including additional child tax credit):
- If your total income will be between $15,000 and $42,000 ($20,000 and $65,000 if married), enter "1" for each eligible child plus **1 additional** if you have three to five eligible children or **2 additional** if you have six or more eligible children.
- If your total income will be between $42,000 and $80,000 ($65,000 and $115,000 if married), enter "1" if you have one or two eligible children, "2" if you have three eligible children, "3" if you have four eligible children, or "4" if you have five or more eligible children. . . **G** ___

H Add lines A through G and enter total here. **Note:** This may be different from the number of exemptions you claim on your tax return. ▶ **H** ___

For accuracy, complete all worksheets that apply.
- If you plan to **itemize or claim adjustments to income** and want to reduce your withholding, see the **Deductions and Adjustments Worksheet** on page 2.
- If you have **more than one job** or are **married and you and your spouse both work** and the combined earnings from all jobs exceed $35,000, see the **Two-Earner/Two-Job Worksheet** on page 2 to avoid having too little tax withheld.
- If **neither** of the above situations applies, **stop here** and enter the number from line H on line 5 of Form W-4 below.

──────────────────── Cut here and give Form W-4 to your employer. Keep the top part for your records. ────────────────────

Form **W-4**
Department of the Treasury
Internal Revenue Service

Employee's Withholding Allowance Certificate
▶ For Privacy Act and Paperwork Reduction Act Notice, see page 2.

OMB No. 1545-0010

2002

1 Type or print your first name and middle initial   Last name

2 Your social security number

Home address (number and street or rural route)

3 ☐ Single ☐ Married ☐ Married, but withhold at higher Single rate.
Note: If married, but legally separated, or spouse is a nonresident alien, check the "Single" box.

City or town, state, and ZIP code

4 If your last name differs from that on your social security card, check here. You must call 1-800-772-1213 for a new card. ▶ ☐

5 Total number of allowances you are claiming (from line H above **or** from the applicable worksheet on page 2) **5** ___

6 Additional amount, if any, you want withheld from each paycheck **6** $ ___

7 I claim exemption from withholding for 2002, and I certify that I meet **both** of the following conditions for exemption:
- Last year I had a right to a refund of **all** Federal income tax withheld because I had **no** tax liability **and**
- This year I expect a refund of **all** Federal income tax withheld because I expect to have **no** tax liability.
If you meet both conditions, write "Exempt" here ▶ **7** ___

Under penalties of perjury, I certify that I am entitled to the number of withholding allowances claimed on this certificate, or I am entitled to claim exempt status.

Employee's signature
(Form is not valid unless you sign it.) ▶

8 Employer's name and address (Employer: Complete lines 8 and 10 only if sending to the IRS.)   Date ▶

9 Office code

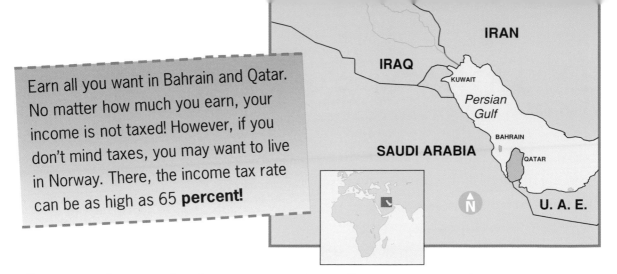

Earn all you want in Bahrain and Qatar. No matter how much you earn, your income is not taxed! However, if you don't mind taxes, you may want to live in Norway. There, the income tax rate can be as high as 65 **percent!**

After December 31 of each year, an employer figures out several amounts related to its workers' pay. These amounts include the total amount of money workers earned at that job, and the amounts withheld for federal income tax, **Social Security** tax, and **Medicare** tax. If your state has a state income tax, your employer records the amount withheld for that tax too.

All this information is recorded on a "Wage and Tax Statement," known as a W-2 form. Employers are required to complete these forms and send copies to workers by January 31. Also, your employer sends a copy of the forms to the IRS as well as your state's department of revenue.

All taxpayers must complete a tax return form. Filling in the information on the form helps determine how much tax a person owes and how much he or she has already paid. Taxpayers must submit the form, along with a check or money order for any tax due, on or before April 15. If you have already paid more money than you owe, the government will send you a tax refund check.

Tax Dollars as Revenue

The **federal** government depends on taxes from a variety of sources for its **revenue**. **Income** taxes provide nearly half of the money the government uses to pay its bills. A little more than one-third of the money comes from payments made to **Social Security** and **Medicare**.

Sources of Federal Revenue

Individual income tax, 48 **percent**

Social Security, Medicare taxes, etc., 34 percent

Corporate income tax, 10 percent

Other sources of income including gift, estate, and customs taxes, 4 percent

Excise taxes including taxes on alcohol, tobacco, and transportation, 4 percent

Hair-raising tax

Throughout history, governments have been creative in naming items to be taxed. From 1795 to 1869, people in Great Britain were required to pay a yearly tax on hair powder!

*That from and after May 5, 1795, there shall be raised, **levied,** collected, and paid throughout Great Britain, unto and for the use of his Majesty, his **heirs** and successors, the stamp duty following: every person who shall use, or wear any powder, commonly called hair-powder, ...there shall be charged a stamp duty of one pound one shilling.*

Like the federal government, many states depend on personal income tax for a large part of its revenue. In California, for example, personal income tax accounts for 56 percent of general fund revenue for the state. California's other major sources of revenue include sales and corporate taxes.

Sources of California General Revenue

Individual income tax, 56 percent

Sales tax, 29 percent

Bank and corporate income tax, 8 percent

Excise taxes on alcohol, tobacco, 1 percent

Other, 5 percent

Estate tax, 1 percent

Local governments, including the governments of villages, cities, counties, and parishes, rely on their own mix of taxes and fees. For instance, the city of Chicago relies on a mix of property, income, sales, and utility taxes for its revenue. The city also benefits from fees paid to use city facilities, such as airports and convention centers.

Sources of City of Chicago Revenue

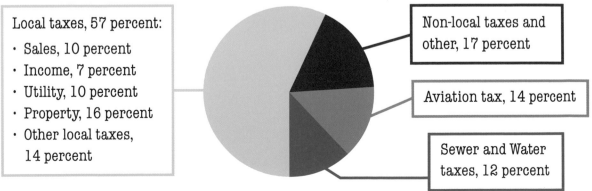

Local taxes, 57 percent:
- Sales, 10 percent
- Income, 7 percent
- Utility, 10 percent
- Property, 16 percent
- Other local taxes, 14 percent

Non-local taxes and other, 17 percent

Aviation tax, 14 percent

Sewer and Water taxes, 12 percent

Tax Dollars at Work

The **federal** government spends the money its receives from taxes on a variety of programs. The greatest part of federal **expenditures,** or spending, goes to provide **Social Security, Medicare,** and Medicaid benefits. These programs assist **retired** workers and poor or disabled people who need medical care. Other spending goes to pay for defense, education, emergency assistance, interest on the national **debt,** and benefit programs designed to assist individuals and families.

Federal Expenditures (typical)

Social Security, **23 percent**

Medicare and Medicaid, 19 percent

Entitlement programs (food stamps, child nutrition, veterans' pensions, federal retirement programs, unemployment insurance, etc.), 12 percent

Defense, 16 percent

Non-defense (education, training, science, housing, etc.), 19 percent

Interest payments on government loans, 11 percent

Money from federal government, state, and local sources helps families and businesses recover from disasters. The Federal Emergency Management Agency (FEMA) sent in workers to help people after a major winter ice storm struck Missouri in 2002.

California is typical of most states—its greatest single expense is kindergarten to twelfth-grade education. Other big expenses include help for people with special needs and assistance for higher education, including college.

California Expenditures

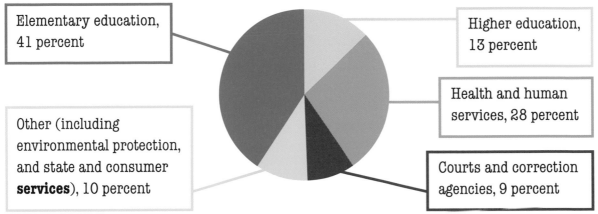

Elementary education, 41 percent

Higher education, 13 percent

Health and human services, 28 percent

Other (including environmental protection, and state and consumer **services**), 10 percent

Courts and correction agencies, 9 percent

As do most cities, Chicago spends much of its **revenue** for fire and police protection. The city also spends money on services such as building roads, paving streets, collecting garbage, delivering water, and sewer services.

City of Chicago Expenditures

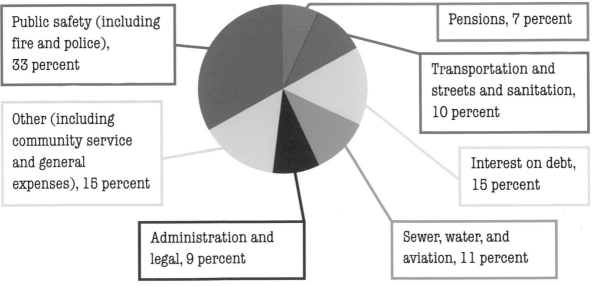

Public safety (including fire and police), 33 percent

Pensions, 7 percent

Transportation and streets and sanitation, 10 percent

Other (including community service and general expenses), 15 percent

Interest on debt, 15 percent

Administration and legal, 9 percent

Sewer, water, and aviation, 11 percent

Property Taxes

Most cities, such as Chicago, rely on property taxes for part of its **revenue,** but the cities themselves do not collect property taxes. Also, some city school systems are not paid for by the city. Instead, both of these responsibilities belong to the local county government, in this case, Cook County.

Cook County collects taxes from property owners based on the value of the property they own. The county then sends the money it collects to different agencies. These include county agencies such as the Cook County Forest Preserve District and the Cook County Water Reclamation District.

If the taxed property is located in Chicago, the county also sends tax money to agencies such as the City of Chicago, the Chicago Board of Education, and the Chicago Park District. If the property taxed is located in Cook County, but not in Chicago, the county sends the money to the appropriate agencies in that town or suburb.

The taxing districts listed on this county tax bill are related to the address of the property being taxed.

Address of property

Taxing districts

2001 Second Installment Property Tax Bill

Amount due if paid by 11/01/2002:
$ **1,131.28**

Property Index Number (PIN)	Volume	Code	Tax Year	(Payable In)	Township
		478	2001	(2002)	LAKE VIEW

If received:	Amount due is:
(on time) 11/01/2002	1,131.28
(late) 11/02/2002 – 12/01/2002	1,148.25
(late) 12/02/2002 – 1/01/2003	1,165.22

Do not double pay. Pay only the correct amount. By state law, the penalties for late payments are 1.5% per month.

	1st Installment Tax due 3/1/2002	Penalty	2nd Installment Tax due 11/1/2002	Penalty
=	0.00 +	0.00 +	1,131.28 +	0.00
=	0.00 +	0.00 +	1,131.28 +	16.97
=	0.00 +	0.00 +	1,131.28 +	33.94

Thank you for your 1st installment payment of   1,062.56
Last payment received on   03-01-02
This tax bill may be used to pay at any LaSalle Bank through 1/1/03.

Property location and classification for this PIN (To update, contact the Cook County Assessor's Office at 312-___-____)
___ W WINDSOR AVE   CHICAGO IL 60640 5752   Property Classification 2-99

Taxing District	2001 Tax	2001 Rate	Pension	2000 Tax	2000 Rate
SCHOOL FINANCE AUTHORITY	63.60	0.223		60.85	0.223
CHICAGO PARK DISTRICT	155.72	0.546	6.55	151.99	0.557
PARKS-MUSEUM/AQUARIUM BOND	5.99	0.021		4.09	0.015
BOARD OF EDUCATION	1,067.83	3.744		1,013.44	3.714
CITY OF CHICAGO	421.54	1.478	197.93	408.76	1.498
CHICAGO TIF WILSON YARD	0.00	0.000		0.00	0.000
CHICAGO LIBRARY FUND	45.35	0.159		44.20	0.162
CHICAGO COMM.COLLEGE DIST	87.56	0.307		84.86	0.311
WATER RECLAMATION DIST	114.37	0.401	7.41	113.24	0.415
FOREST PRESERVE DIST	19.11	0.067	.85	18.83	0.069
COUNTY OF COOK	155.44	0.545	43.35	165.09	0.605
COOK COUNTY HEALTH FACIL.	57.33	0.201		59.76	0.219
(DO NOT PAY THESE TOTALS)	2,193.84	7.692		2,125.11	7.788

How was my tax calculated?

2000 Assessed Value
=   14,296
Property Value   89,350
Assessment Level   X 16%
2001 Assessed Value
=   14,296
2001 State Equalization Factor
X   2.3098
2001 Equalized Assessed Value (EAV)
=   33,021
Less Homeowner Exemption
–   4,500
Less Senior Citizen Exemption   0
Less Senior Freeze Exemption
–   0

2001 EAV After Exemptions
=   28,521
2001 Local Tax Rate
X   7.692%
2001 Total Tax
=   2,193.84
First Installment (Due 3/01/2002)   1,062.56
Second Installment (Due 11/01/2002)
+   1,131.28
2001 Total Tax (Payable In 2002)
=   2,193.84
Payment data from warrant records in the Cook County Treasurer's Office.

KEEP UPPER PORTION FOR YOUR RECORDS

FRED FOLLANSBEE
CHICAGO IL

Maria Pappas

IF YOUR MORTGAGE COMPANY PAYS YOUR TAXES FROM ESCROW, DO NOT DOUBLE-PAY YOUR TAXES.

Cook County Property Taxes

Chicago Taxing Districts	Evanston Taxing Districts
County of Cook	County of Cook
Cook County Health Facilities	Cook County Health Facilities
City of Chicago	City of Evanston
School Finance Authority	School Finance Authority
Water Reclamation District	Water Reclamation District
Forest Preserve District	Forest Preserve District
Chicago Community College District	Oakton College District
Chicago Park District	Evanston General Assistance
Parks-Museum/Aquarium Bond	North Shore Mosquito Abatement
Board of Education	Consolidated Elections
Chicago Library Fund	North Suburban Mass Transit District

Chicago and Evanston are two cities in Cook County. Cook County collects property taxes for properties located within the county. The money is then sent to the cities and towns within the county. This table shows some things that the tax money pays for.

Window tax

In the mid-1600s England started a window tax. A tax collector decided how much tax needed to be paid by counting the number of windows in a person's house. This tax left the poor with two options: either they could live in darkness day and night or they could go into **debt** to pay the window tax. Some families chose to brick up their windows or replace them with boards. This tax came at a time when there was also a tax on candles, so some people were left in total darkness. This led to less clean housing and an increase in disease.

There were similar taxes in the United States. The 1798 U.S. Direct Tax was nicknamed the "window" or "glass" tax because the amount of the tax was based on the number of windows in a house. Records of this tax can be found in several Pennsylvania counties.

Taxes and Education

Throughout the United States, a large portion of **federal**, state, and local taxes pays for education. This helps insure that the country has a public school system that can produce educated and informed citizens. Educated and informed citizens form the foundation of a democracy. They are able to identify what assistance and support they need from their government. They can elect people who will work to supply those needs.

One of the earliest examples of American schooling occurred in the Massachusetts Bay **Colonies.** In 1642, the colonies passed a law requiring that parents teach children how to read and write English. Children were also expected to know local laws and religion.

Education in colonial times was different from today's education. Young children learned the alphabet and numbers. In addition, girls learned cooking and sewing. At schools similar to today's elementary schools, students learned the language of the colony as well as reading, writing, arithmetic, and religion. All the teachers were men; all the students were boys.

The Massachusetts Bay Colonies passed a law that required children and apprentices to be taught how to read and write English.

In 1647, the General Court of the colonies passed a law requiring every township of 50 households to appoint and pay for an elementary school teacher. The law also required that every township of 100 households hire a **secondary** teacher as well. These laws show that the colonial government felt its citizens should be educated and that the government should have some control over education. More importantly, the laws show that citizens of the Massachusetts Bay Colonies felt that taxes could be used to pay for education.

Know It

After the Revolutionary War, states were responsible for educating citizens. However, the federal government continued to play a role in the development of schools.

The authors of the U.S. Constitution did not mention education as a federal responsibility. Therefore, the responsibility for education passed to the individual states. However, by passing the Northwest Ordinances in the 1780s, the federal government actively encouraged the development of state-supported education. The federal government indicated that education was "necessary to good government and the happiness of mankind."

Hornbooks

Colonial schoolchildren did not have books like the books used in schools today. Instead, colonial students studied one page at a time. Because paper was expensive, each page or sheet of paper was glued to a small wooden paddle. In order to keep the paper clean, a thin piece of cow's horn covered it. This gave the books their name, hornbooks. Hornbooks usually contained the alphabet, some simple words, and religious sayings or proverbs.

The Northwest Ordinances

In the 1780s, the Northwest Ordinances required each of the territories to set aside the **income** from the 16th section of each township for the support of education (a township was 6 square miles [15.5 sq. kilometers], subdivided into 36 sections). At the time of the ordinances, the income from the section would have been crops. The Northwest Ordinances included land that eventually became the states of Michigan, Illinois, Wisconsin, Indiana, and Ohio.

State

Section

6	5	4	3	2	1
7	8	9	10	11	12
18	17	**16**	15	14	13
19	20	21	22	23	24
30	29	28	27	26	25
31	32	33	34	35	36

County

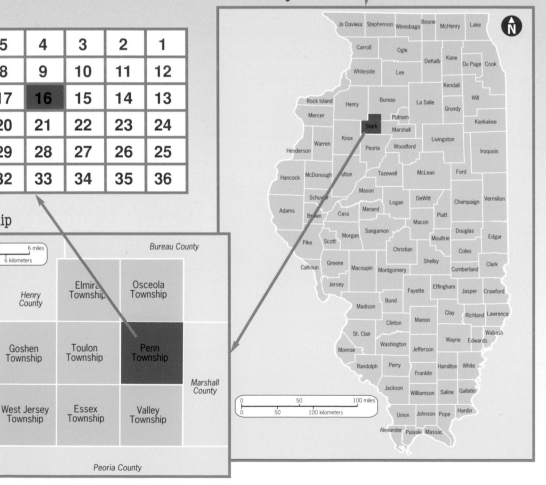

Township

At the end of the 1700s, the leaders of the new United States began to stress that education was important for citizenship. They felt that good government could exist only if the governed give their permission to be governed. Therefore, education should include information that an informed citizen would need. Finally, the leaders hoped that education would promote a sense of nationalism, that is, a sense of an American identity and loyalty to America. Taxes helped make education possible.

Benjamin Franklin

Thomas Jefferson

Noah Webster

Franklin, Jefferson, and Webster

Three leaders whose ideas shaped America's educational system were Benjamin Franklin, Thomas Jefferson, and Noah Webster. Franklin was in favor of a useful and scientific education. He started a publication called *Poor Richard's Almanac*. It emphasized values such as frugality and hard work.

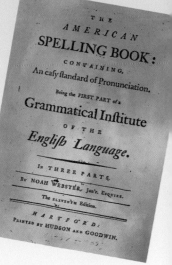

At the end of the 1700s, Thomas Jefferson wrote the "Bill for the More General Diffusion of Knowledge." The educational goals of the bill stated that the government was responsible for providing schools, schools should produce citizens who could read, and public schools should be free from religious instruction.

Noah Webster's influence centered on the growth of the American English language and American culture. He wrote an American spelling book to replace the English books that American schoolchildren were using. He also wrote an American Dictionary.

During the 1800s, the way people made products changed. Simple machines used at home or in rural areas were replaced by power-driven machines located in factories, often in cities.

During the 1800s, American society experienced great changes. At the beginning of the century, most people lived in **rural** areas and worked in farming and farm-related jobs. By 1900, most people lived in cities and worked in manufacturing and industry. As a result of this change, America needed workers who could at least read and write.

The state governments allowed different areas of the state to set up local school districts and encouraged these districts to **levy** taxes to support the schools. In about 1850, the Common School came into existence. Most state governments wanted to keep overall control of education while giving day-to-day control of schools to local government. In order to do this, the state governments allowed sections of the state to form school districts.

In general, Common Schools included grades one through eight, each in its own classroom with its own teacher. Both males and females were teachers. Subjects included reading, writing, arithmetic, and spelling. Some schools also offered history, geography, and public speaking.

Each school district had a locally-elected school board. This school board ran nearly every aspect of the local schools. In addition, the school board was responsible for making sure schools followed the state's educational policies.

The state **legislatures** required that school districts provide education for all children living within the district's boundaries. The states passed **legislation** that would encourage the local school districts to impose taxes to pay for the public schools. If a district raised money for its schools through taxes, the state would give the district additional funds for education. Most districts chose to support their schools by starting a property tax.

Why support schools?

Some supporters of Common Schools reinforced the idea that the country needed educated citizens, others saw public education as a way for their children to advance. Still others recognized the public schools as a way to introduce common values, loyalties, and a sense of American ideals in children from different ethnic backgrounds.

People who did not support the schools tended to be owners of factories, mines, and plantations. They felt they could not afford to lose cheap child labor. Other people wanted their children taught in their own language, religion, and traditions. Above all, people who did not want to pay taxes for the support of education opposed the schools.

Paying for Today's Education

By 1918, all states offered public school education. In addition, all children were required to attend school. Few exceptions were made.

Today there are more than 1,500 public school districts in the United States. A school district may include a single school or many schools. Although state governments set up the school district boundaries, local governments—such as county, village, or city—manage the day-to-day operations of the schools.

Know It

Federal, state, and local taxes help pay for free public education in the United States.

Education and the constitution

State constitutions of most of the 50 U.S. states provide for free, public education. This means that all children should have an equal opportunity to receive free, quality education from kindergarten to grade twelve. The Texas constitution says:

> A general diffusion [spread] of knowledge being essential [important] to the preservation [protection] of the **liberties** and **rights** of the people, it shall be the duty of the **Legislature** of the State to establish and make suitable provision for the support and maintenance of an efficient system of public free schools.

In the 1999–2000 school year, the average number of students in a public middle school was 595. The average number of students was 446 for public primary schools and 752 for public high schools.

42

School aid

During the 1997–1998 school year, governments spent about $326 million in school aid or an average of $6,000 for each public school student in pre-school through grade twelve. Federal funds provided seven **percent** of the money, state sources provided 48 percent, and local and intermediate sources provided 45 percent of the total.

School Revenue Sources

Federal tax money (7¢ Federal)	State tax money (48¢ state sources)	Local tax money (45¢ local and other sources)
head start, school lunches, textbooks, school health services	general funds, construction and repair of school buildings	teacher's **salaries,** books, transportation, salaries of repair and maintenance workers

In many school districts, local property taxes remain the main source of school **revenue.** Many people feel this method is not fair because property wealth is not equally distributed across communities.

Communities with expensive homes and valuable properties bring in more tax dollars than poorer communities with lower property values. This means schools in communities with higher property values are more likely to have computers, well-stocked libraries, and enough of the equipment and supplies needed.

Follow Your Money

Find out if your city collects a sales tax and the amount of the tax. You might be able to do this by checking cash register receipts from a grocery store, a video store, or a shoe store. You might try to find the information with an adult on your city's website on the Internet.

Cause and effect

Many cities depend on sales tax for **revenue.** If a great number of people in the city lose their jobs, they have less money to spend. If people spend less, the city collects fewer sales tax dollars. If people move out of the city the result is the same—the city collects fewer sales tax dollars. Sometimes the amount of money a city takes in shrinks so much that the city does not have enough money to pay for city services.

The newspaper is a good place to find out about taxes. Newspapers often report tax increases and decreases.

MAYOR URGES PLAN FOR DRASTIC CUTS AND TAX INCREASES

RESPONSE TO FISCAL WOES

New York Would Reduce Size of Police Force and Close Eight Fire Companies

By MICHAEL COOPER

Mayor Michael R. Bloomberg outlined his plan yesterday to pull New York City through its worst fiscal crisis since the 1970's by raising taxes significantly while simultaneously cutting the size of the police force, closing fire companies, reducing new day care slots for children and shutting centers for the elderly.

New York Times
Late Edition
New York: Today, partly sunny, mild, high 61. Tonight, cloudy, rain arrives, low 44. Tomorrow, rain, heavy at times, windy, high 48. Yesterday, high 56, low 40. Weather map, Page C8.
NEW YORK, FRIDAY, NOVEMBER 15, 2002
75 CENTS
$1 beyond the greater New York metropolitan area.

Little Headway In Terror War, Democrats Say

Bin Laden Tape Is Cited — New F.B.I. Alert

By DAVID JOHNSTON and ERIC LICHTBLAU

WASHINGTON, Nov. 14 — American intelligence agencies came under renewed attack in Congress today for failing to find Osama bin Laden, with the increasing certainty that he is still alive prompting senior Democratic senators to brand the effort to dismantle Al Qaeda as a failure.

Even as Bush administration officials took the F.B.I. to task for a warning issued on Wednesday about possible attacks on hospitals, the F.B.I. today issued a vague and alarming alert to state and local law enforcement agencies. The alert warned that this week's message, apparently from Mr. bin Laden, plus intelligence reports and recent overseas strikes by Al Qaeda, had raised the threat of attacks.

The alert was no specific information.

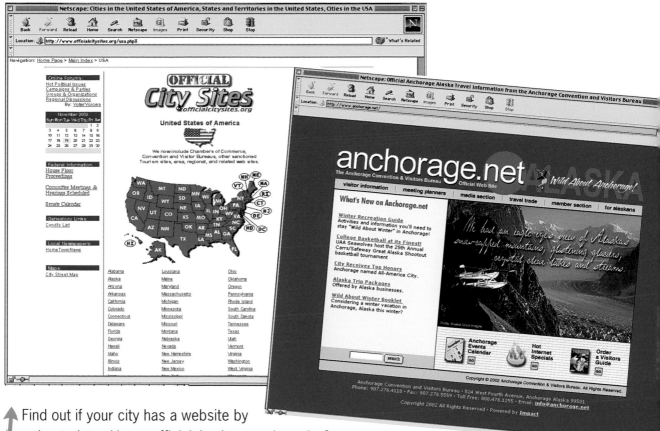

Find out if your city has a website by going to http://www.officialcitysites.org/usa.php3.

Once you know how much the city collects in taxes, find out how much, or what **percent,** of the money your city keeps. If your city does not keep all of the sales tax it collects, find out who else gets the tax money.

See if you can follow the money to find out what **services** are paid for with the sales tax you pay at the nearby grocery store.

Glossary

amendment legal change to a law or group of laws

barter to trade by exchanging goods or services instead of money

boundary something that points out a limit or end; dividing line

civil rights rights that all citizens have in a government; for example, all citizens have the right to be represented in government

colony territory settled by people from other countries who still had loyalty to those countries

debt something that is owed

economy use or management of money

employer person that hires and pays others to do work

excise tax on certain goods or services

expenditure act of spending

extended family family including parents, children, and other close relatives

federal describing a union of states that share a government

good thing that can be bought or sold

heir person who inherits or has the right to inherit property after the death of its owner

income money earned through work

inheritance money or property received upon the death of another

insurance contract by which someone guarantees for a fee to pay someone else for the value of property lost or damaged

knight man who served a king or lord as a soldier

legislation process of making laws

legislature people with the power to make laws

legitimate according to law

levy to bring about or collect

liberty freedom to do what one pleases

linen strong cloth made of flax

lord man of high rank or manor owner

Medicare government program of medical care, especially for older people

merchant person who buys goods in one place and sells them in another, often a different country

Parliament law-making body of the United Kingdom

percentage part in relation to the whole

privilege right or liberty granted as a favor or benefit, especially to some and not others

proportional size, number, or amount of one thing or group of things as compared to that of another thing or group of things

Prussia historical region in Northern Germany, boarding the Baltic Sea

reform improve by correcting errors or defects

regulation rule, order, or law

repeal officially withdraw or reverse

representation act as an agent of

resource source of wealth

retire give up one's work or business

revenue money collected by a government

Roman Empire lands and people under the rule of ancient Rome

rural countryside

salary set amount of money paid for work over a certain period of time

secondary school after elementary

service work done for another or others

Social Security government program of retirement benefits

tariff moneys collected on imported or exported goods

toll charge, especially for crossing a bridge or road

unconstitutional not in agreement with a constitution

withhold to refuse to give, grant, or allow

More Books to Read

Burkett, Larry (ed.). *Money Matters for Kids.* Chicago: Moody Press, 2001.

Giesecke, Ernestine. *Dollars and Sense: Managing Your Money.* Chicago: Heinemann Library, 2003.

Valliant, Doris. *Personal Finance.* Broomall, Penn.: Chelsea House, 2001.

Index

ability to pay 6, 19, 20

barter 8

city
  expenditures 33
  revenue sources 31

death tax 11
direct tax 6, 14, 24

estate tax 6
excise tax 6, 18, 20, 26

fair tax 24–25
federal
  expenditures 32
  revenue sources 30
feudalism 10–11
FICA 22–23

head tax 8, 11

income 8
indirect tax 6
inheritance tax 6

knights 10

license fees 8

Magna Carta 12–13
Medicaid 32
Medicare 22–23, 32

progressive tax 26, 27
property tax 7, 26
proportional tax 27

regressive tax 26

sales tax 6, 9, 19, 26, 31, 45
Social Security 22–23, 29, 32
social security cards 25
Stamp Act 14–17
state
  expenditures 32
  revenue sources 31

tariffs 15, 16, 18
tax
  death tax 11
  direct tax 6, 14, 24
  estate tax 6
  excise tax 6, 18, 20, 26
  fair tax 24–25
  head tax 8, 11
  indirect tax 6
  inheritance tax 6
  progressive tax 26, 27
  property tax 7, 26
  proportional tax 27
  regressive tax 26
  sales tax 6, 9, 19, 26, 31, 45
Tea Act 15
1040 forms 29
1040EZ forms 29

W-2 forms 28
W-4 forms 28
Withholding Certificates 28